BRANDON, 18 MOS.

SIERRA, 4 YRS.

THIS BOOK BELONGS TO

_____

We dedicate this book to all of our Memory Makers contributors whose fun and amazing pages, albums, and ideas are the inspiration behind these pages.

PAGE 114

PAGE 85

Contents

PAGE 14

PAGE 32

PAGE 74

PAGE 46

PAGE 81

PAGE 48

Blanketed in...

DANIEL. 1½ YRS.

ANNA 2½ YRS.

SASHA 2 YRS.

...Love

MY CHILDREN QUICKLY BECAME
ATTACHED TO THE SOFT BLANKETS
AUNT PAM HANDMADE FOR THEM
WHEN THEY WERE BORN.

Introduction

Run! Climb! Eat! Play! No! Mine! Nap! Read! These words ruled our everyday lives during toddlerhood. With all three of my kids now entering new phases of development, I look back at these years with a blur. Energy, joy and surprises blessed our days, as they continue to do so, and I'm so grateful for the photos and memories captured during this time.

Between the ages of one and five are the whirlwind years of accomplishments. Learning to walk, communicate, explore, and much more. These years revealed my kids' personalities and defined their characteristics. Scrapbooking these special moments and milestones imprints a memory and creates a foundation of confidence and love.

For this book we had over 2,000 page ideas to sort through. What helped our selection process was to ask the question "Is this page unique to the life of a toddler or is it a great page that happens to have a picture of a toddler on it?" There were so many amazing pages, and in the end, it was very difficult to narrow it down to what would fit on these pages.

We have featured many unique page ideas for recording everything—from your child's daily rituals, playtime, and best friends to potty training, trips, and social activities. In addition, we have included the stories behind the pages, as well as ideas for recording growth and those all-important milestones and "firsts." Lastly, we offer how-to steps for special techniques—such as paper piecing and color blocking—as well as numerous theme album ideas, patterns and reproducible art to help you get started.

One thing I've realized though, through raising kids, is that it sure helps to approach the toddler and preschool years with a sense of humor. As you glean ideas from this book and reminisce, I hope you find a smile on your face and your wheels start turning about the pages you want to create or the pictures yet to take.

Michele

BLANKETED IN...LOVE
MY KIDS THEN & NOW
(SEE PAGE 125)

MICHELE GERBRANDT
FOUNDER OF *MEMORY MAKERS* MAGAZINE

1 Getting Started

Early childhood years are energetic times, filled with humorous explorations, innocent chaos, and ever-changing contradictions. With young children, you may feel too busy to create a scrapbook album that captures the essence of toddler and preschool life, but a little organization and inspiration will help you stay on the right path despite the detours that young children bring. Here, we will show you how to get started on building those first pages in five easy steps.

3 CREATE CATEGORIES

Write categories for your photos and memorabilia on sticky notes. Categories can be in chronological order or even modeled after the chapters in this book. See the photos and memorabilia checklists on page 13 for ideas. You can add or remove categories as you go.

4 ORGANIZE PHOTOS & MEMORABILIA

Sort photos and memorabilia into your categories. As you work, jot down memories that the photos inspire on sticky notes or on the back of the photos with a photo-safe wax pencil to help with journaling. After sorting photos into your chosen categories, put each category into chronological order.

5 STORE PHOTOS & NEGATIVES

Store sorted photos and negatives in a safe environment while you work on your album. Use only 100% acid-, lignin-, and PVC-free negative sleeves, storage binders, and photo boxes.

1 SET UP A WORK AREA

Set up a well-lit work surface stocked with sticky notes, a pen, your photos, and an acid-free photo box.

2 DECIDE ON A THEME

Decide if your album will be an ongoing, continuous "life" album or a theme album that tells the story of specific events from early childhood. See pages 38-39, 65, 78-79, 87, 110-111, and 116 for theme album ideas.

ALBUMS

Albums come in three-ring binder, post-bound or strap-style, allowing you to remove, add, or rearrange pages as needed. Spiral-bound albums make great theme albums for children or as a gift. The quantity and physical size of your photos and memorabilia will help determine the size of album you need.

SCISSORS & PAPER TRIMMER

Keep a pair of sharp, straight-edge scissors and a paper trimmer at hand. Also, use decorative scissors for creative edges on photos and mats. Turn decorative scissors over to achieve a varied cutting pattern.

2 Basic Tools & Supplies

Once you've chosen a theme and organized your photos and memorabilia, you're almost ready to create your first page. But first, gather the following tools:

ADHESIVES

Use scrapbooking adhesives, such as glues, tapes, and mounting corners, that are labeled "acid-free" and "photo-safe." Rubber cement, white school glue, and cellophane tape contain chemicals that can harm photos over time.

PAPERS

Acid- and lignin-free decorative papers are available in countless colors and patterns. Use these versatile papers for a background, an accent, or to mat or frame photos.

DESIGN ADDITIONS

Unique design additions can give a page theme continuity. These can include stickers, die cuts, memorabilia pockets, photo corners, and more. Shop with a list of needed supplies and some photos to match colors and avoid any unnecessary spending.

PENCILS, PENS & MARKERS

Journaling adds the voice and pertinent facts to your scrapbook. A rainbow of journaling pens and markers, with a variety of pen tips, make fancy penmanship a snap. Pigment ink pens are best because of their permanence. Photo-safe pencils and wax pencils can be used for writing on the back and front of photos.

RULERS & TEMPLATES

Use rulers and templates to crop photos or trace shapes onto paper, to cut decorative photo mats, or to create your own die cuts.

3 Create a Layout

FOCAL POINT

Choose an enlarged, matted, unique, or exceptional photo for a focal point on the page to help determine an eye-pleasing layout. This is where the eye will look first. Other photos on the page should support this image.

BALANCE

Place your photos on a one- or two-page spread. Large, bright, or busy photos can feel "heavier" than others so move the photos around until the page no longer feels weighted or lopsided while leaving enough space for journaling.

COLOR

Choose background and photo mat papers and design additions that complement the photos, making them stand out, rather than compete for attention. Sometimes less is more. Too much color can be distracting.

Crop-n-Assemble

4

CROPPING

Photo cropping can add style, emphasize a subject, or remove a busy background. See Memory Makers Creative Photo Cropping for Scrapbooks *for hundreds of cropping ideas.*

MATTING

Single or layered paper photo mats focus attention and add balance to a page. Use a paper trimmer, decorative scissors, a template, or freehand cut a mat, leaving a border around the photo.

MOUNTING

Mount photos on your page with double-sided tape or liquid adhesives for a permanent bond. Paper or plastic photo corner triangles allow for easy removal of photos, if needed.

5 Journaling

The stories behind the photos are details that can be lost forever if they're not included on your page. Start with one, or a combination, of the simple journaling styles shown below:

BULLETS
Start with the basics of who, what, when, and where in bullet form.

CAPTIONS
Expand on bulleted information with complete sentences, allowing for more creative expression.

JOURNALING TIPS

- ◆ *Write freehand in light pencil first, then trace with ink.*
- ◆ *Journal on a separate piece of paper, cut it out, and mount it on the page.*
- ◆ *Use pencil to trace a lettering or journaling template on the page, then trace with ink.*
- ◆ *Print journaling on your computer. Crop, mat, and mount journaling or trace the journaling onto your page using a light box.*
- ◆ *Journal onto die cuts or mats, write around your photos in curved lines, or turn paragraphs into shapes.*
- ◆ *Photocopy and color the lettering patterns on pages 118-119 for quick page titles.*
- ◆ *Use the journaling checklist on page 13 to help bring your photographic story to life.*

STORYTELLING
Give details about those in the photo at the time the photo was taken. Include everything from clothing, background items, mood, and conversation—perhaps even the weather!

QUOTES, POEMS & SAYINGS
Search for your subject on quotation-related Web sites, in poetry books, in the Bible, even on T-shirts!

- Christian

- Age 3

- March 1997

- Playing peek-a-boo

I See You!
Sweet Christian
Age 3
Playing peek-a-boo
in his tunnel of
puzzle blocks on a
cold snowy day
March 1997

Do I See You!
Yes, Christian
Just came into view!

Oops, gone again,
But wait and see,

I'll bet his smile
comes back for me!

Age 3
March 1997

The Complete Page

It's easy to get caught up in the avalanche of scrapbooking products available, but it's important to stay focused on the purpose of scrapbooking when completing a page—to preserve your youngster's memories. With that in mind, make sure your page has the five basic elements of a great scrapbook page: photos, journaling, complementary color, effective design, and long-lasting construction.

Peek-A-Boo!

I See You! The cold and snow kept Christian inside this March day. But it didn't stop him from having fun. He used his puzzle blocks to build a tunnel, then had fun peeking out to pose for these photos. At 3, he is such a sweet, fun-loving little boy. 1997

CHRISTIAN, 3 YRS.
Photos Cheryl Rooney, Lakewood, Colorado

Checklists

As your child quickly maneuvers through the toddler and preschool years, you will have lots of photos, memorabilia, and stories to record. Use these lists as a basic framework for organizing your keepsakes.

- ☐ Being a "little helper"
- ☐ Being "artistic"
- ☐ Daily routines:
  - Bath time
  - Brushing teeth
  - Grooming
  - Mealtime
  - Reading
  - Sleeping
  - Waking up
- ☐ Favorite things (see page 123)

- ☐ Funny faces
- ☐ Growth
- ☐ Holidays
- ☐ Illnesses and boo-boos
- ☐ Messes
- ☐ Milestones and firsts (see page 102)
- ☐ Organized activities (see page 93)
- ☐ Personality traits (see page 34)
- ☐ Playtime, dress-up and pretend play
- ☐ Potty training
- ☐ Preschool, nursery, and Sunday school

- ☐ Professional portraits
- ☐ Travel and outings
- ☐ Visits to doctor and dentist
- ☐ Your child with:
  - Family and siblings
  - Family pets
  - Favorite people
  - Friends and playmates
  - Teachers, coaches, and caregivers
  - Visitors to home

MEMORABILIA

Keep your child's most interesting and important memorabilia, as well as those your child cherishes the most. Consider photographing an overabundance of memorabilia for your album, if necessary. See page 93 for tips on de-acidifying memorabilia.

- ☐ Artwork
- ☐ Birthday invitations, cards, decorations, wrapping paper samples
- ☐ Certificates, ribbons, and awards from organized activities
- ☐ Color-copied favorite book covers
- ☐ Color-copied wallpaper and fabric swatches from bedroom
- ☐ Copy of doctor and dentist notes
- ☐ Early childhood heritage photos of relatives for family tree (see page 122)
- ☐ Growth and development records
- ☐ Hair clippings
- ☐ Hand and foot prints
- ☐ Labels from favorite foods
- ☐ Letters to child from family and friends
- ☐ List of gifts
- ☐ Preschool, nursery, and Sunday school mementos
- ☐ Souvenirs from travel and outings
- ☐ Time capsule souvenirs

JOURNALING

Keeping a daily journal can be demanding with a toddler in the house. Instead, jot tiny notes on a calendar to add to the scrapbook later. Some things you might wish to record:

- ☐ Beloved books, rhymes, songs and games
- ☐ Family tree information (see page 122)
- ☐ Favorite things at a given age (see page 123)
- ☐ Funny things your child says and does
- ☐ Height and weight for growth chart (see page 124)
- ☐ Milestones and firsts (see page 102)
- ☐ Growth and loss of baby teeth
- ☐ Personality and character traits (see page 34)
- ☐ What you like about your child and why
- ☐ Assign an adjective to each letter of your child's name

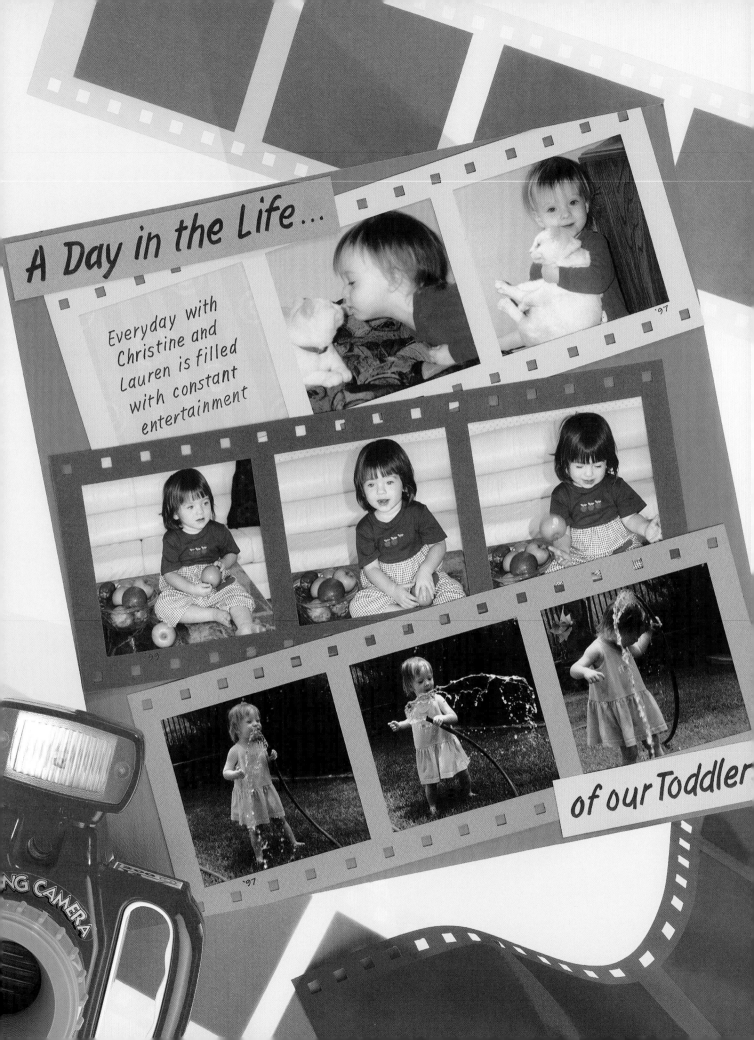

A Day in the Life...

Everyday with Christine and Lauren is filled with constant entertainment

of our Toddler

A Day in the Life

IT ISN'T THE GREAT BIG

PLEASURES THAT COUNT THE

MOST; IT'S MAKING A

GREAT DEAL OUT OF THE

LITTLE ONES.

—JEAN WEBSTER

Her eyes fly open in the morning and flutter begrudgingly shut at night. In between, a toddler is a force of nature, a swirling mass of energy and emotion. She is a baby still, but empowered with walking and words; she wants to know more. Are hot dog bits more fun to eat or throw? Why walk when you can run, run, run! Establishing predictable routines—from warm bubble baths to cozy times reading together to regularly scheduled meals around the family dinner table—helps your toddler focus her enthusiasm and settle down when she needs to. And you get a chance to catch your breath. In the meantime, try to keep your camera loaded with film at all times and your scrapbooking supplies handy!

A DAY IN THE LIFE...
CHERI O'DONNELL, ORANGE,
CALIFORNIA
(SEE PAGE 125)

ADAM, 2 YRS.

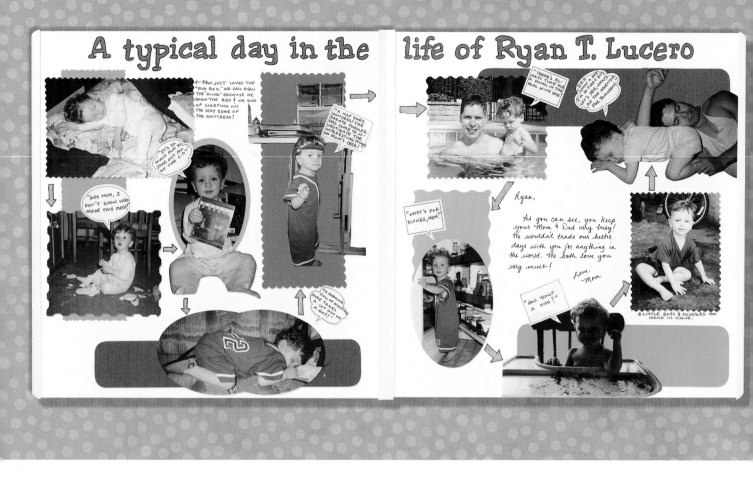

A Typical Day

PHOTOJOURNAL A BUSY DAY

Debbie decided to document "one of those crazy days" of running after her busy toddler. Document a day by first cropping photos with decorative scissors or into silhouette shapes. Cut paper strips; trim with decorative scissors or round corners. Layer photos and strips on page with conversation "bubble" stickers (Mrs. Grossman's). Add journaling and humorous toddler thoughts. Complete with freehand-drawn title and arrows leading a path around the page.

Debbie Lucero, Colorado Springs, Colorado

Geometry Lesson

SHAPE A COLORFUL BORDER

Janie's page design is both easy to make and educational. To create a page full of simple shapes, adhere geometric stickers (Mrs. Grossman's) around page to create border. Crop photos into basic shapes; mat on colored paper. Freehand journal title and captions.

Janie Thomas, Blakely, Georgia

Child's Play

CHILDREN ARE NOT

SO DIFFERENT THAN KITES...

CHILDREN WERE CREATED TO FLY.

—GIGI GRAHAM TCHIVIDJIAN

Toddlers don't need power suits or briefcases to get ahead in their careers. They play for a living! Yet every form of play serves an educational purpose. The lesson might be theoretical physics, say, building block towers vs. gravity. Or it might be role-playing: today a firefighter, tomorrow a ballerina. Preschool artwork, done in vibrant paint and crayons, shows how they see the world. Toddlerhood favorites give insights into emerging personalities, while ride-on toys encourage developing motor skills. Join right in on healthy games of imaginary play to let your child know that you know it's only a game and that you enjoy it too. Devote many pages to your youngster's world of play to serve as a rewarding reminder of his or her creative young mind.

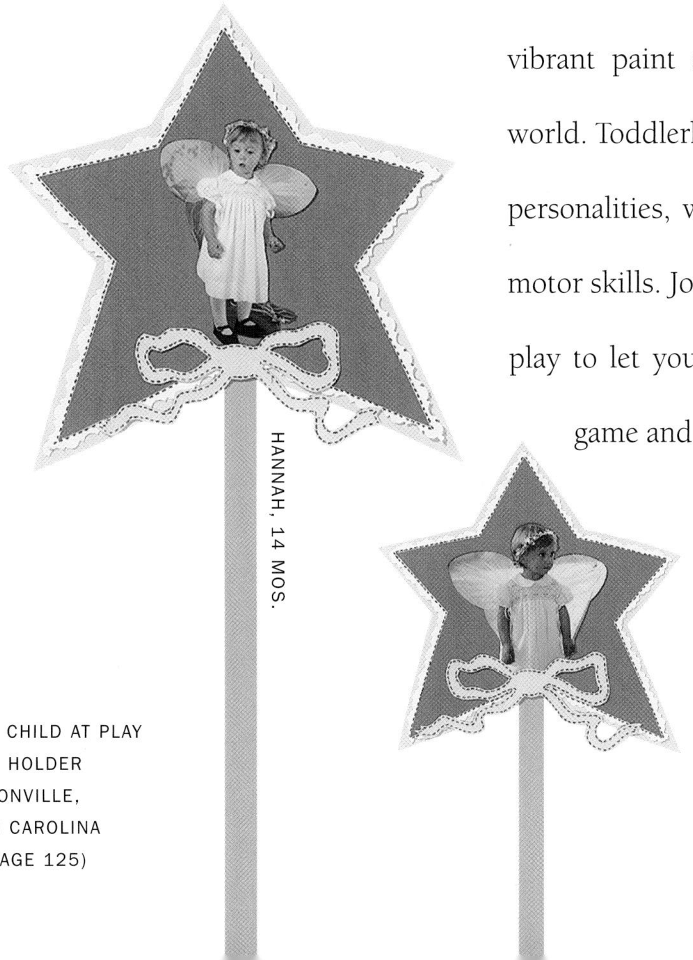

HANNAH, 14 MOS.

I AM A CHILD AT PLAY
KAREN HOLDER
JACKSONVILLE,
NORTH CAROLINA
(SEE PAGE 125)

Playtime

MAKE TOY-SHAPED PHOTO MATS

Nancy ties together various photos of her daughter playing by framing the photos in toy shapes. Photocopy and size telephone and stacking ring toy patterns (see page 120) to serve as a photo template. Crop photos to fit and mat. Silhouette crop toys from photo scraps and layer in bottom corner. Title and journal with red pen.

Nancy Chearno-Stershic, Bel Air, Maryland

Playtime

STACK UP PLAYFUL PICTURES

The random placement of the rings on Trish's page mimics the rambunctious activity of her children at play. First, crop photos and mat on bright colored paper; round corners of photos and mats. Photocopy and enlarge ring toy and ring patterns (see page 120); transfer to colored paper and cut out. Layer photos; slide ring shapes over corners of photos and mount. Adhere title letters (Creative Memories) and colored dot stickers (Mrs. Grossman's). Complete page by outlining photos, detailing toy and journaling with black pen.

Trish Tilden, Westmont, Illinois

REAGAN, 3 YRS.

MITCHELL, 3½ YRS.;
SPENCER, 2 YRS.

Sticky fingers,
dirty face
Rugs and pillows
out of place.
Cars and tractors
here and there,
blocks and boats
everywhere.
Gold and Silver
have I none,
but worth a million
are my sons.

--Ruth Joy

I dropped my dolly
in the dirt
I asked my dolly
if it hurt
and all my dolly said is
wa-ah, wa-ah, wa-ah

BRITTANY, 18 MOS.

HANNAH

an object in motion stays in motion

Hannah, An Object in Motion...
CAPTURE THE WHIRL OF ACTIVITY

Photos of Brenda's daughter in nonstop action are
shaped into a colorful, geometric design that illustrates
Sir Isaac Newton's law of motion. Start by cropping the
center photo freehand or with a template. Crop surround-
ing photos into geometric shapes, matching one side of
each photo to the center photo. Triple mat on colored
paper. Mount center photo with foam spacers between
matting to add dimension. Freehand crop directional triangles and mount around photos. Trace and crop font
title and lettering (*Bold Script Alphabets: 100 Complete
Fonts* by Dover Publications); mount on page.

Idea and Photos Brenda Gottsabend, Canton, Ohio

Future Farmers

CAPTURE A TIMELESS MOMENT

Vicky caught a glimpse of her two boys' future one afternoon when she snapped these beautiful photos. Complementary paper colors for the background and matting enhance the natural setting of the photos. Freehand draw title letters, mat and trim with decorative scissors (Fiskars).

Vicky Clayton,
Maymont, Saskatchewan, Canada

Alt Computer Whiz

PROGRAM KEY-PUNCHING FUN

Jana's son, a true 21st-century kid, was introduced to the computer at an early age, and has loved it ever since. Complement photos with keyboard paper (Hot Off The Press) for the background. Cut a 2½" border strip from brown paper; adhere title letters (Creative Memories). Mat photos; trim with decorative scissors (Family Treasures).

Jana Tafelski, Grand Haven, Michigan

FUTURE BUILDER

Constructing a page around this photo of
Amanda Bott's (Hendersonville, Tennessee)
architect-in-training began as her son's love
for building blocks grew. It's fun to imagine
your child's future career, based upon the
types of toys and activities he favors most,
and then build a page around that "career."
Twenty years from now, your scrapbook page
may prove to have been a prediction!

CHRISTIAN, 3 YRS.

Paging Dr. Bozeman

REMEMBER ROLE-PLAYING FUN

Pretend play is an entertaining and cru-
cial part of toddler development. Debbie
recorded her son, the budding doctor,
attending to his first patient. Start the
page with a patterned paper background
(Keeping Memories Alive) and mat
cropped photos with darker patterned
paper (Keeping Memories Alive), leaving
space for journaling. Finish with a cus-
tom-made paper doll (Barbra's Dolls)
and sticker letters (Provo Craft).

Debbie Bozeman, Rochester Hills, Michigan

Jammin

HIGHLIGHT A CLASSIC TODDLER ACTIVITY

Yvonne silhouette-cropped her daughter's classic "banging on the pots and pans" photos for this
groovy page design. Circle cut graduated paper rings in three different colors; mount as shown.
Mat silhouette-cropped photos on paper circles; mount as shown.
Add punched flowers (Family Treasures), letter stickers (Making Memories),
journaling and ink dots around letters to finish.

Yvonne Nickerson, Mashpee, Massachusetts

Jared's First Painting
FRAME PHOTOS WITH FLAIR

Jennifer framed photos of her little artist creating his first masterpiece with artistic flair. Create your own "gallery" by cropping photos and mounting on page. Frame with colorful paper scraps or hand drawn designs. Freehand cut paper-pieced artist from paper scraps. Adhere crayon and paint-related stickers (source unknown). Complete page with photo captions and title.

Jennifer Gould, Costa Mesa, California

Artist at Work
CREATE A SCRAP MASTERPIECE

While capturing her son's creative efforts, Jolene puts her cropping leftovers to use. She calls her finished product, "The Frugal Format: Pages for Pennies." Leftover patterned paper strips line the bottom of the page and provide a background for the title. Title blocks, which are actually the sticky paper leftovers from sticker letters, are adhered to square decorative paper scraps. Paint splats are crafted from leftover pieces of maple and oak leaf die cuts (Ellison).

Jolene Wong, Walnut Creek, California

Mommy's Little Artist
PRESERVE THE CREATIVE PROCESS

Splashes of color enliven Donna's daughter's first paintings. To feature the artwork of your budding artist, layer red paper over gingham paper (Frances Meyer). Freehand cut palette and brush. Freehand crop large photo and circle cut two smaller photos; mat with freehand "color splotch" shapes. Adhere artist stickers (Stickopotamus). Add title and journaling with black pen.

Donna Pittard, Kingwood, Texas

Busy Little Hands
FEATURE CLAY CREATIONS

Playing with Play-doh® is a favorite activity for Caroline's daughter and husband! Begin by backing photos with single and double mats layered on a yellow speckled background (Westrim) trimmed with border sticker strips (me & my BIG ideas). Layer double matted title lettering (Cock-A-Doodle Designs) partially over photo. Complete page with journaling using template (EK Success) to make wavy lines.

Caroline Lebel, Toronto, Ontario, Canada

Color My World
CROP A CRAYON BACKGROUND

Larger-than-life crayons make a colorful background for photos of Diane's little artisans. To make crayons, cut an 8½ x 1⅞" strip of colored paper and a 11⅞ x 1⅞" strip of darker paper in the same color family. Cut one end of the darker strip into a 2¼" point to form tip. Mount light strip atop darker, pointed strip. Make five more crayons. Crop photos; mount on crayon background. Add sticker letters (Frances Meyer) and journaling.

Diane Bottolfson, Sioux Falls, South Dakota

ELISE, 3 YRS.

Hot Wheels

RECORD CREATIVE CAR COLLECTION

Melissa's mind raced into action when her son was looking for a way to beat the boredom blues. Together, they outlined Alex's body with his car collection, making a "Car Alex." Blue cardstock provides the background for silhouette-cropped car outline and cropped photos matted on red or white paper. Auto stickers (Current) matted on white paper build on the page's theme. Print title lettering, journaling and mat.

Melissa Abbe, Vancouver, Washington

Love My Blocks

BUILD ON CONSTRUCTIVENESS

Mitzi was so inspired by her son's elaborate block designs, she decided to craft her own. Creatively shaping scraps into geometric shapes can reflect a child's creative designs and add playful fun to your pages. Small title letters (Provo Craft) keep the focus on the design element and photos.

Mitzi Stuart, Paducah, Kentucky

TV Time

SPOTLIGHT YOUR STAR

Andrea displays her favorite "couch potatoes" on their own TV screen! To make a television, cut a 10¼ x 8" rectangle from taupe cardstock. Cut a gray 8 x 6¾" rectangle for TV screen; round corners. To make dials, punch large black circles and mat with jumbo punched gray circles; adhere. Mat a gray rectangle with rounded corners to black rectangle for speaker; adhere. Draw details with silver ink and add journaling.

Andrea Wheatcraft, Frankfort, Kentucky

ELIJAH, 4 YRS.; CHLOE, 12 MOS.

Little Dolls

DOCUMENT CHERISHED DOLLS

Angi created an appropriately titled layout with photos of her twins and their favorite dolls. Begin with pink and blue paper over gingham paper (The Paper Patch), leaving a 1" border for the background. Mount photos with white photo corners (Boston International) over layered mats. Circle cut and partially silhouette crop photo; mat on solid paper. Cut title letters from template (EK Success) on polka dot paper (The Paper Patch); double mat on colored paper. Freehand craft doll head and hair for letter "O"; punch bows (McGill). Punch flower bouquets: daisy, circle and birch leaf (Family Treasures), large flower (All Night Media), teardrop (EK Success), mini sun (Marvy Uchida) and small daisy (Carl). Layer to create bouquet; mount. Print journaling, mat on solid paper and add pink triangles at two corners.

Angi Holt, St. George, Utah

all of my FAVORITE things
pickles · pull toys · cheese ·
trains · raisins · horses ·
whales · pickles · juice ·
race track · horses · crackers
little wooden toys · pickles
animals · juice · dogs · cheese
trains · cereal · pickles ·
whales · juice
Kellogg's
Raisin Bran
Honey Maid
Dole
RAISINS

All of My Favorite Things

SHOWCASE FAVORITE TOYS AND FOODS

To help remember the details of her toddler's favorite things, Michele photographed them. To create this page, start with patterned paper (Gussie's Greetings) for the background and add double-matted photos, cropped in ovals and squares. Create page title with ⅝" wide strip with matted oval centered; journal with black pen.

Michele Fischer, Aberdeen, Washington

JESSICA, 2 YRS.

Going Places in My Car

CREATE A RIDE-ON ROADWAY

(BELOW) Catherine's son takes to the road on this two-page spread. To create your own road, start with blue background paper. Use template (Accu-Cut) to cut road, photos and journaling block; shade top of road with gray chalk. Double mat large photo. Use template (Accu-Cut) for title and mat. Cut car and decorations from template (Accu-Cut); assemble. Punch 38 black small squares; mount on white cardstock for banner and flags. Cut doll and clothing from template (Accu-Cut); assemble. Adhere doll to car, placing vellum behind windows and doll. Mount on page. Finish spread with journaling.

Catherine Schulthies for Accu-Cut, Fremont, Nebraska

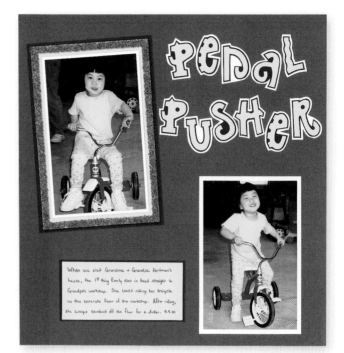

ZACH, 11 MOS.

Pedal Pusher

FEATURE A FAVORITE PASTIME

(FAR UPPER LEFT) Lois captures her daughter's spirit soaring while riding her favorite tricycle in Grandpa's workshop. Start with the title using a lettering template (EK Success); double mat on black and white paper. Single mat one photo and triple mat another. Add Beedz™ (Art Accents) for texture on the triple mat. Complete page with journaling.

Lois Rodgers, Lowell, Arizona

Get Ready, Get Set, Go!

SILHOUETTE TODDLER TRANSPORTATION

(UPPER LEFT) Mary gathered photos of her little one on the go, showing some of the ways he takes to the road. To begin, freehand cut "road" with decorative scissors (Fiskars); draw white dashed line. Silhouette crop photos; layer on road. Adhere character (Suzy's Zoo), transportation and road sign (both Mrs. Grossman's) stickers. Stamp grass background (Posh Impressions). Add title sign and journaling.

Mary Ellefson, Freeport, Illinois

Caution, Future Driver

POST SIGNS OF THE TIME

(UPPER RIGHT) When Jeanette's son got behind the wheel with his "cell phone," she saw warning signs all over the place! Freehand cut street signs and mount atop strips of black paper for sign posts. Double mat photos. Freehand title and letter street signs.

Jeanette Goyke, China Township, Michigan

Creating Shadows

From hand-puppet animal shadows cast upon walls to the long end-of-summer shadows cast by bridges and trees, shadows intrigue all of those who are young at heart. If you have photos with great shadows, you can easily re-create the shadows as one-of-a-kind page embellishments. Simply make a paper-pieced version of the object in your photo that casts a shadow, then trace around it on black paper to create the shadow. To achieve the most realistic shadow based on the direction of the implied light source, experiment with proper placement of the shadow on the page beneath its paper-pieced counterpart before adhering to page.

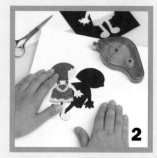

Me and My Shadow

EXPAND ON A PHOTO ELEMENT

Judy loved the shadows of her daughter at play, so she carried the look onto her scrapbook page. To create this look, double mat photos, offsetting the second mat. Freehand draw a hopscotch grid. "Dress" a paper doll (Stamping Station) with paper-pieced hair and clothing to match your child's. Follow the steps to the right to make the doll shadow and shadowed title letters traced and cut from a lettering template (Provo Craft).

Judy Diehm, San Antonio, Texas

DOLL SHADOW

1 *Trace around paper doll onto black paper; cut out (Figure 1).*
2 *Layer "shadow" doll at an angle beneath paper doll (Figure 2), using the light source direction of the shadow in your photo(s) as a guide for proper doll shadow placement, and adhere.*

SHADOWED LETTERS

3 *Adhere black "shadow" letters on page first, then layer red letters atop, slightly lower and to the left (Figure 3). In this manner, the black shadow letters will fall in the same direction as the black doll shadow, staying true to the direction of the implied light source.*

Me and My Shadow
RE-CREATE SHADOW PLAY

Chris created a clever page depicting her son's fascination with his shadow as light streamed through a window. Start with an orange background. Create window by layering the scene from the background out, beginning with blue paper for sky. Add hill, tree, cloud and butterfly stickers (Mrs. Grossman's) and sun die cut (Dayco). Freehand cut window frame and sill out of yellow patterned paper (source unknown); add cat sticker (Mrs. Grossman's). Freehand cut large sunray out of rainbow paper (Paper Adventures) and craft paper doll (Accu-Cut) with shadow; adhere. Crop photos, mat on black paper, and trim corners as shown to achieve shadow effect. Finish pages with title letter squares, matted the same as photos; adhere sticker letters (Provo Craft) and hand draw the rest of title.

Chris Peters, Hasbrouck Heights, New Jersey

It's Fun to Imagine That...
BUILD ON AN ACTIVE IMAGINATION

Michelle was inspired to create an imaginative page with photos of her daughter playing in a box. Begin with pink background. Create the foursquare look by adding two green rectangles to background, as shown. Silhouette crop photos. Freehand cut title block. Cut journaling blocks with decorative scissors (Fiskars). Title and journal with black pen. Complete page with transportation stickers (Mrs. Grossman's); punch "thought dots" with circle hand punch.

Michelle Siegel, Lake Worth, Florida

MITCHELL, 21 MOS.

All in a Day's Work

Toddlers mimic Mommy and Daddy in pure "monkey see, monkey do" fashion. But work doesn't always have to be, well, work. Folding clothes can easily become an impromptu fashion show or dress-up play. Early chores and working together set a productive pattern for life. Just set reasonable goals and be there to capture your damsel in distress or your courageous little superhero.

Penny, nickel, quarter, dime....Penny, nickel, quarter, nickel dime...the very first time! I just earned an allowance for

COLIN, 4 YRS.

CHORE LIST

✓ Fold kitchen towels
✓ Pick up toys
✓ Dirty clothes to laundry

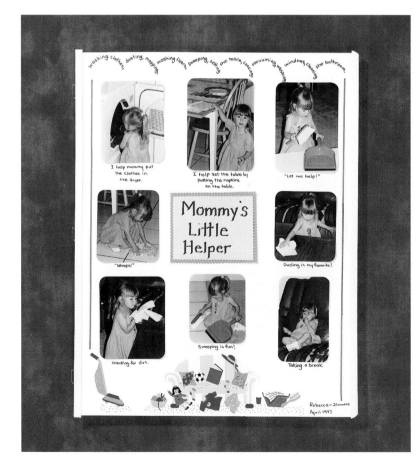

Mommy's Little Helper
SHOW OFF HOUSEKEEPING SKILLS

Cleaning the house is no chore for Michelle's daughter, and helps take the load off of Mom! Start by creating a border with descriptive words scalloped across top of page using a decorative ruler (Creative Memories) for guidance. Layer furniture clutter and object stickers (Mrs. Grossman's) across bottom of page. Draw thick lines down sides of page with pen. Crop photos; round corners and mount. Create title block with solid paper matted and trimmed with decorative scissors. Complete page with title lettering and photo captions.

Michelle Siegel, Lake Worth, Florida

Mommy's Helper

PRESERVE A TIMELESS TRADITION

Cara shares the baking of cookies with her daughter, and has captured a timeless feel with hand-tinted black-and-white photos. Mat and mount photos on solid paper trimmed with decorative scissors (Fiskars) over patterned background paper (The Paper Company). Craft paper dolls (Stamping Station); freehand draw clothes and baking accessories out of patterned (Everafter), solid and specialty (Paperwood by Lenderink) papers. Punch title squares (Family Treasures); outline with metallic pen and adhere sticker letters (Paper Adventures). Create journaling block with stamp (Colorbök) on gingham paper (Keeping Memories Alive); mat and trim with decorative scissors.

Cara Wolf-Vaughn, Carversville, Pennsylvania

Mommy's Helper

ADD PAPER-PIECED DETAIL

Melissa's daughter is a great help around the house, especially when she's willing to do the dirty work! Begin with soft-colored patterned paper (The Paper Patch) for background. Crop photos; single and double mat on solid and patterned (Keeping Memories Alive) paper. Craft paper-pieced vacuum from pattern (*Paperkuts*); adhere sticker letters (Provo Craft). Print title (*Lettering Delights CD* by Inspire Graphics); double mat. Print decorative corners; trim to size and mount.

Melissa Abbe, Vancouver, Washington

JAMI'S STORY

Sometimes the best part of parenting comes when you see the world anew through your child's eyes. Jami experienced this joy with her 15-month-old son, Travis, as their family was preparing to move into a new home. The house needed lots of work, including a fresh coat of paint inside and out. Travis soon became best buddies with the painting company owner, Todd, as he painted the house's interior a sunny yellow.

One fall evening following move-in, Jami took Travis out into their backyard to enjoy the view of a full harvest moon. As they watched the golden orb sitting low in the sky, Travis suddenly blurted out, "Todd paint a moon!" Jami was amazed that her son could connect their wall color with the moon, remember the painter, and that he could even articulate the thought.

"I am so grateful to have this bright, creative spirit by my side to help me discover the world again," says Jami. "I look forward to many more months and years to come of painted moons, animal clouds, lemonade rain and wishing stars."

Jami McCormick, Louisville, Colorado

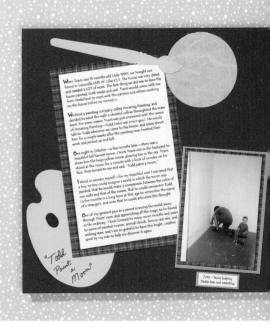

THEO, 2 YRS.

"Mom, I Ate the Bills"

HIGHLIGHT LITTLE HELPER'S MISCHIEF

Lisa's daughter thought it would be better to eat the bills, rather than pay them! To capture your little helper's mischief, double and triple mat photos and layer on background paper. Create title letters using template (Cut-It-Up) on specialty paper (Sandylion). Punch flowers (All Night Media, Family Treasures). Adhere postmark stickers (Stickopotamus) and bill memorabilia. Finish page with journaling.

Lisa Shupe, Ben Lomond, California

Men at Work

GROW A GRASSY BORDER

Little boys love to work with Dad, especially when they have their own tools. Begin with a blue patterned paper (Provo Craft) background, layered with a 2½" grass paper (Hot Off the Press) border sliced every ⅛". Silhouette crop photos; layer over grass. Crop additional photos; mat on red paper. Freehand cut sign for title; layer over brown paper strip for post and detail with black pen. Add silhouette-cropped bugs from paper (Current). Complete with title, journaling, and pen details.

Idea Cara Stroud, Midland, Texas
Photos Pennie Stutzman, Broomfield, Colorado

Pretty in Pink

THEME TOGETHER COLORFUL CLOTHES

A collection of colorful outfits comes together for Allie to feature her daughter all dressed up. To begin, crop photos; mat on a variety of patterned papers (Close To My Heart, The Paper Patch) and round corners of photos and mats. Adhere appropriately colored stickers (Frances Meyer, Mrs. Grossman's) and sticker letters (Making Memories) around photos.

Allie Littell, Mebane, North Carolina

Brittany Anne

SHOW OFF YOUR LITTLE DOLL

So many clothes, so little time for Charla's darling paper doll daughter. To make a quick-and-easy page, silhouette crop photos of "doll" and clothes. Add small white paper clothes "tabs" outlined in black ink. Display on page as desired.

Charla Campbell, Springfield, Missouri

Disney® Prêt-à-porter

CATALOG FAVORITE CLOTHES

Cindy collected various photos left over from previous layouts and found a common thread...all had her daughter dressed up in Disney "ready-to-wear" fashions. Create a catalog-themed layout by cropping photos and matting on paper. Create "mouse ear" decoration with large circle punch mounted over freehand cut "ears;" detail with pen. Freehand cut sewing accessories; detail with black pen. Freehand draw title from logo; journal with black pen.

Cindy Kitchin, Naslemoore, California

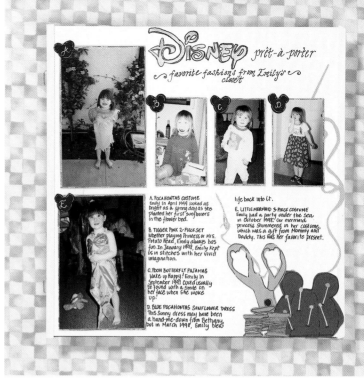

Poor Girl

PRESERVE TODDLER WARDROBE

Cheri's quick-and-easy page serves a dual purpose—it effectively ties together several unrelated photos of her daughter while successfully documenting the youngster's wardrobe. First, adhere one uncropped photo directly on page to serve as a focal point. Add freehand cut hangers with title and journaling, as shown. Silhouette crop remaining photos; place randomly on page. Finish with stamped swirl (Biblical Impressions) designs.

Cheri O'Donnell, Orange, California

Hats!

FEATURE COLLECTION WITH STYLE

Candid photos caught Emily's kids raiding her closet and trying on all of her hats. Begin with yellow and blue papers, cut into geometric shapes, layered over a soft-colored background. Silhouette and square crop photos. Create title and journaling blocks in geometric shapes on ivory paper; lightly dust around edges with pink chalk (Craf-T Products). Freehand creative lettering; detail with pens and color with chalks. Add journaling.

Emily Tucker, Matthews, North Carolina

Fashion Footwear

SHOW OFF FASHION FLAIR

There's no such thing as a fashion faux pas in the eyes of a toddler, as shown in Tamara's comical fashion layout. To create your own stylish page, crop photos; mat on white paper. Freehand draw photo corner details and outline mat with black pen. Highlight fashionable photo details with silhouette cropping. Layer photos and title blocks on page. Adhere camera die cut, photography-related stickers and photo corner stickers (Creative Memories) to complete the design.

Tamara Ruby, McKinney, Texas

Color Blocking

Use blocks of color to add a dynamic dimension to your page. The clean lines of color blocking add just the right splash of color, which is a great substitute for pattern and texture. Experiment with tried-and-true, as well as uncommon, color combinations for a truly contemporary effect.

See Jack Go

CRAFT A CONTEMPORARY DESIGN

As you can see from our cover art, bold colors, combined with silhouette-cropped photos of busy Jack, work together to form an energetic color-block design. To make a similar 8½ x 11" scrapbook page spread, begin with white paper for background. Then follow the steps below to create the pages.

1 *Freehand cut six 4" squares, six 4 x 4¾" rectangles, and five ½" wide strips from colored and patterned papers; trim to fit pages. Use bold-colored markers to shade some of the squares and strips (Figure 1) and set aside.*
2 *Carefully silhouette crop 7 or 8 selected photos with scissors (Figure 2). Cut slowly, following the child's outline, and be careful around hair and facial features. Random photos of hands, feet, even a child's mouth will lend a more abstract touch to the layouts.*
3 *Assemble color block shapes in a pleasing scheme and layer with silhouette-cropped photos. Apply an adhesive (Figure 3) that is flexible enough to use on tiny areas of silhouetted photos to ensure adherence prior to mounting on color blocks. Finish pages by adhering hand-cut, slightly uneven paper strips atop color block seams and adding bold-colored journaling. Note: For a 12 x 12" scrapbook spread, cut six 4" squares and six 4 x 7½" rectangles with ½" strips in between or six 4" squares and six 4 x 6" rectangles with 2" strips in between.*

Two Little Shoes

PRESERVE A SPECIAL PAIR OF SHOES

Lynn cherished how proud her son was of his
favorite pair of shoes, so she made an ink impression
of one. The page was highlighted with a shoe-related
poem (author unknown) and two cropped and matted photos trimmed with decorative scissors. A small
star punch was used to embellish the page.

Lynn Butler, Palm Bay, Florida

Superboy

SPOTLIGHT A SUPER-TODDLER

Linda captures her son in superhero style as he flew
in and out of different outfits, dressing up in the
flash of an eye. Spotlight your superhero on a red
background surrounded by bold colors. Crop photos, mat on yellow paper. Freehand cut star burst,
arch, and zigzag matting for silhouette-cropped
photo. Create title and captions in shadowed letter
style with colored pens. Complete page with journaling in blue pen.

Linda Wright, Hartford, Connecticut

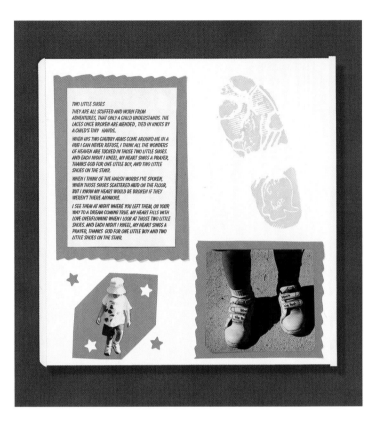

I spy Hew in a flannel shirt,
a hard hat,
a hammer,
a pile of dirt!

I spy Hew trying to hide,
a soccer ball,
a bouncing frog,
a yellow slide!

Now that you have
looked at Hew,
Go back and find
something new!

sun   star
             triceratops
ball
        arrow
gloves mail
        lotion
        hat

"I Spy" Album

Children love looking for hidden objects and solving
riddles, as seen in the popularity of Scholastic &
Cartwheel Books® "I Spy" book series. Tracy's
"I Spy Hew" album is a homemade, toddler-themed
version with personalized rhyming text that leads her
son to find objects hidden on the scrapbook pages.

"Hew just loves it!" says Tracy. An added bonus—
the very nature of an "I Spy" album allowed Tracy to
use many leftover and extra photos and paper scraps
that might have otherwise gone unused. In addition,
a wide array of colorful stickers allowed her to illustrate the rhymes with ease.

Tracy Haynes, Boynton Beach, Florida

"I SPY" VARIATIONS

Photograph numerous still-life collages composed
of a hodgepodge of your child's favorite things
(see page 123 for ideas), create photo collages
of cropped and silhouetted photos of family
and friends, or create a photo collage of
animal pictures from the zoo. Then write
text that leads your child to find certain
objects, people or animals.

1997

A year of family, friends, and fun!

Left page: Tony comes to visit • Jake starts preschool • Rachel & Daddy go for a swim • Sydney/Sidney • Rachel says goodbye to Bryan • Fourth of July fun at the Aberbook's • Crazy Uncle Richie • Rachel makes her favorite sandwich (peanut butter) all by herself! • Sydney gives Jake a kiss

This page: Hangin' out at the Camhi's • Kindergarten friends come over to play with Rachel • Playing at the park with baby Talia • Swingin' in the backyard • Jake's tries to catch flying money at a spring carnival • Lauren and Jake splash splash in the bath • Mommy turns 35 • Rachel holds baby Talia for the first time • Alex gives Jake some basketball pointers • Mommy and Jake have some photo fun!

Family & Friends

THERE ARE ONLY TWO

LASTING BEQUESTS WE CAN

HOPE TO GIVE OUR

CHILDREN. ONE OF THESE IS

ROOTS; THE OTHER WINGS.

—HODDING CARTER

The world of our toddlers starts in the hearts of family and friends. They're the people who love our little ones simply because they are. Starting with Mom and Dad, then radiating out to relatives and friends, a toddler's ties spread to all who will play and cuddle and tussle a bit. A toddler has other connections too, to those who came before and those who will follow. It's never too early to start "family tree" pages for your toddler, showing not just family but friends, also. Photos and journaling are especially vital here to ensure that memories of faces and good times will last forever.

1999:
A YEAR OF FAMILY,
FRIENDS & FUN!
KELLY ANGARD
HIGHLANDS RANCH,
COLORADO
(SEE PAGE 125)

LYNDSEY, 2 YRS., TYLER, 4 YRS.

There Are Little Eyes Upon You

HIGHLIGHT A SPECIAL RELATIONSHIP

Photos of a special father-son relationship are accompanied by a meaningful poem (author unknown) to create a page that brings tears to Tammy's eyes. Begin with black cardstock background. Crop photos with decorative scissors (Family Treasures) or oval template (Family Treasures) before matting on red paper. Print poem on tan paper, then crop with scalloped heart template (Family Treasures) and mat on red paper. A punched train (Family Treasures) is the final embellishment.

Tammy Layman, Sterling Heights, Michigan

Once Upon a Time

JOURNAL A MAGICAL MOMENT

Kelly captures her daughter's dress-up play with Daddy in fairy tale fashion using storybook journaling. First, crop photos and mat on solid paper trimmed with decorative scissors. To help carry out the theme, add a color-copied scene from an actual storybook, if desired. Mount photos and art on page. Finish with title, journaling and pen work in black ink.

Kelly Angard, Highlands Ranch, Colorado

2 of a Kind
RECORD DRESS-ALIKES

Laura's page illustrates the day she and her daughter dressed alike. Create this colorful border using a filmstrip border punch (Family Treasures) around edges of colored background paper and weave ¼" red paper strip through holes. Adhere background paper to page. Cut ½" strips of polka dot paper for inside border; adhere to background paper. Double mat larger photos with red and polka dot paper and trim with decorative scissors. Frame single photo with heart die cut (Creative Memories). Layer polka dot and solid color sticker letters (Making Memories) to add dimension to title. Add heart stickers (Mrs. Grossman's) and journaling to complete the page.

Laura Elliott, Seaford, New York

LOOK, DAD!

For the little boy who dreams of growing up to be like Daddy, slipping on the shoes is the easy part! Elizabeth Barnes of South Federal Way, Washington, captured her son standing tall in his dad's boots.

JOHNNY, 3 YRS.

BEN, 1½ YRS.

Get Down and Get Dirty

UNITE TWO GENERATIONS

Color and black-and-white photos unite two generations of
Linda's family playing in the mud! To begin, cut 1⅛" strips of
plaid paper (Hot Off The Press); mount on outer page edges.
Mount black-and-white photos; add photo corners cut from
plaid paper. Crop color photos; double mat with solid paper.
Freehand draw title letters; mount on paper squares. Tear brown
paper pieces for journaling to complete title. Add dot detail
around title letters and journaling with black fine tip pen. Cut
mud splats from template (Provo Craft); mount on page.

Linda Cooper, Haines City, Florida

Grandma and Kylen

FRAME A TENDER MOMENT

Rhonda framed a sweet moment between grandma and grandson,
knowing that even though the peaceful memory won't stay with
her son, the photo will. Create a frame by cutting strips of patterned (The Paper Patch) and solid paper with a wavy ruler
(Creative Memories). Print title and journaling on background
paper before layering wavy strips around sides of page. Crop
photo and round corners; mat and trim with decorative scissors.
Adhere flower stickers (Frances Meyer).

Rhonda Thompson, Layton, Utah

In His Sunday Best

"DRESS" PAPER DOLL TO MATCH PHOTO

Pamela highlights heritage photos of her husband's family dressed in their Sunday best. Black paper provides a striking background for red and white diamonds, matted, layered, and crossed with silver metallic stickers strips (Mrs. Grossman's). Crop photos with decorative scissors (Family Treasures); mount with embossed photo corners. Paper doll (Accu-Cut), custom "dressed" in outfit to match photos, stands on cobblestone and grass sticker strips (Mrs. Grossman's). Make custom clothes by tracing paper doll outfit pieces on your own paper. Complete page with printed title and journaling, matted over two red rectangles at corners.

Pamela James, Ventura, California

LISA'S STORY

The newborn calf appeared suddenly one morning at Lisa's father's home. Still trailing the umbilical cord, the cow resisted repeated attempts to shoo it back to its mother. The following day, Lisa's dad fed the cow, dubbed Bob (short for "Shish K. Bob"), milk from a baby bottle. Thereafter, Bob circumnavigated the yard as he followed her dad's voice.

Just a few days after Bob's arrival, Lisa's grandfather died. Bob unexpectedly began to kick and bounce around the front yard as the mourners left for the funeral. The cow's unusual behavior reminded Lisa's dad of how his mother Elise, who is also deceased, would bounce around when she was excited. "Bob brought a lighthearted feeling of wonderment and comfort to my father's home during our time of mourning," remembers Lisa gratefully.

About a week after the funeral, the cow disappeared as quickly as he had arrived. Lisa's dad sadly looked for his new companion and later learned a nearby farmer had reunited the calf with his herd. Perhaps Bob knew he had fulfilled his purpose in bringing Lisa's family a hint of joy in their time of need, and so returned to his own family.

Lisa Horst, Sacramento, California

TEN GREAT WAYS TO HELP YOUR GRANDCHILDREN REMEMBER YOU

1 Tell them about your family's history. Make tape recordings of these moments of sharing together.

2 Create something together: build a doghouse, sew doll clothes, or start a scrapbook.

3 Open a savings account and make a tradition of going to the bank and adding to it.

4 Be open to the nicknames your grandchildren choose for you and find a nickname for each of them.

5 Teach a grandchild about the constellations; he'll remember you every time he looks up at the stars.

6 Share your hobbies with them, and help them start hobbies of their own.

7 Read with them, read to them, read together.

8 Plant a garden together. You'll be planting seeds in the present and the future.

9 Let your grandchildren share secrets with you. Be sure to keep them.

10 Write letters, even in this age of e-mail. Your grandchild will treasure them.

GRANDPA JOHNSON
AND DEREK, 3 YRS.

Boys in Blue

CAPTURE RESEMBLANCES

Cathryn created a striking monochromatic layout with special photos of her son and his grandpa. A solid blue background, layered with patterned paper (Hallmark) provides striped matting for photos. Freehand draw and color lettering and journaling; mount on paper squares to enhance the monochromatic mood of the page.

Cathryn Wooton, Richmond, Virginia

Jansen really resembles his Grandpa Wooton with his solid build, blue eyes, his nice hands & his BIG head !

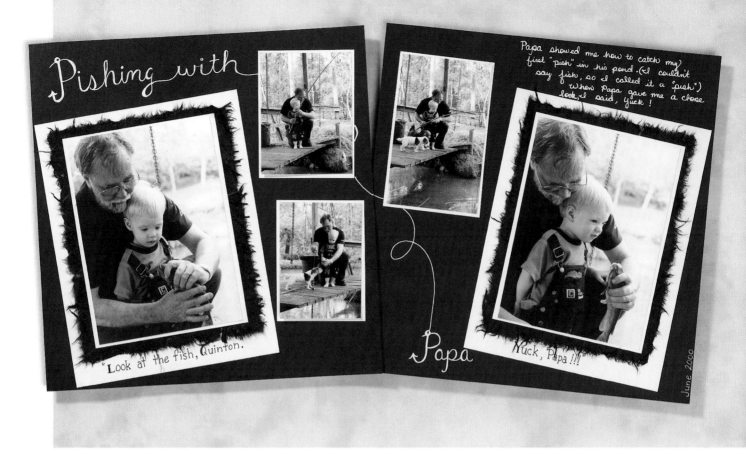

Pishing with Papa

DRAMATIZE A NEW EXPERIENCE

Dramatic black-and-white photos of a first-time fishing
trip tell of a precious day with Grandpa. Patricia kept the
layout simple with matted photos on a black background.
Enlarged photos are featured with torn mulberry paper,
layered between white matting. Freehand title and journaling completes the page.

Patricia Johnson, Cowpens, South Carolina

Making Biscuits

BAKE UP A BONDING TRADITION

Karen passes on the art of making the perfect biscuit by
documenting the special grandmother-granddaughter
bonding and baking time, complete with a recipe to
remember. Create page title by cropping various sized
rectangles to fit mat size. Add letters (Frances Meyer), stickers (Mrs. Grossman's) and stitching lines with pen. Double
mat photos and journaling with patterned and solid paper.

Karen Holder, Jacksonville, North Carolina

Sisters *are flowers in the garden of life*

Sisters

GROW A MEMORY GARDEN

Evangelynn crafted a multi-dimensional garden from photo memories of herself and her sister as youngsters. To begin, freehand cut white strips and assemble picket fence over blue background paper. Jumbo punch (Emagination) photos into flowers; mat on white paper. Freehand cut jumbo daisies from white paper and vellum. Cut daisy center from yellow mulberry paper; layer pieces and mount together at center of flower. Cut green grass paper strips. Freehand cut stems and leaves. Freehand cut ladybugs; detail with black pen. Layer daisies, photo flowers, stems and leaves; mount over fence and under grass strips. To create foldout, jumbo punch additional photos into flowers; tape together on edges and adhere to jumbo flower embellished with jumbo daisy and ribbon tie. Trace printed title (*Curlz* by Microsoft) onto pages; outline in black. Freehand cut dragonfly and bee from solid, metallic (Making Memories) and textured paper (Paper Adventures). Complete page with journaling and pen work.

Evangelynn Lenz, Buckley, Washington

He Ain't Heavy, He's My Brother
PUNCH A RETRO DESIGN

The arrival of another baby boy gave birth to Kenna's retro floral design without looking "girlish." Double and triple mat photos on solid and patterned (The Paper Patch) papers; embellish with mini punched flowers. Punch and layer small and large daisies (Family Treasures), jumbo oval (Emagination Crafts), and ⅛", ¼", ⅝" and 1" circle punches (Family Treasures) to create random flowers. Freehand cut peace signs. Layer elements on page as shown. Trace title letters (Cock-A-Doodle Designs) onto paper squares; overlap and mat on solid paper. Adhere sticker letters (Making Memories).

Kenna Ewing, Parkside, Pennsylvania

Boy Oh Boy Oh Boy
SHOW OFF BOYISH CHARM

Kathy's husband captured this delightfully boyish photo. Begin with patterned background (Keeping Memories Alive). Crop photo, double mat and trim with decorative scissors. Finish with die cut letters (Accu-Cut).

Kathy Hartlaub, Williams Bay, Wisconsin

Brother or...Bully
LIGHTEN UP A SIBLING SQUABBLE

Kelly's ruffian toddler sometimes gets the best of his older brother! Punch characters with stencil-drawn faces (Tapestry in Time) to add comedy. Crop "weapon" photo; triple mat. Title the page with small (Making Memories) and large (Provo Craft) sticker letters.

Kelly Starr, Las Vegas, Nevada

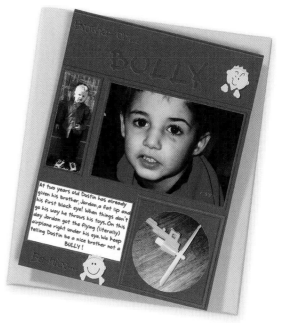

Best Friends
PRESERVE YOUNG SILHOUETTES

Jean paired black-and-white photos with the simplicity of paper silhouettes to create a classic look. Start with a solid colored background. Crop photos with decorative scissors (Family Treasures) on side edges. Add photo corners (Canson) and mount to black mats trimmed with decorative scissors. Silhouette-crop silhouette portraits; trace onto black paper and cut out. Mount paper silhouettes on cream paper. Adhere photos and add journaling. Add pen stroke design to finish.

Jean Guernsey, Brookfield, Connecticut

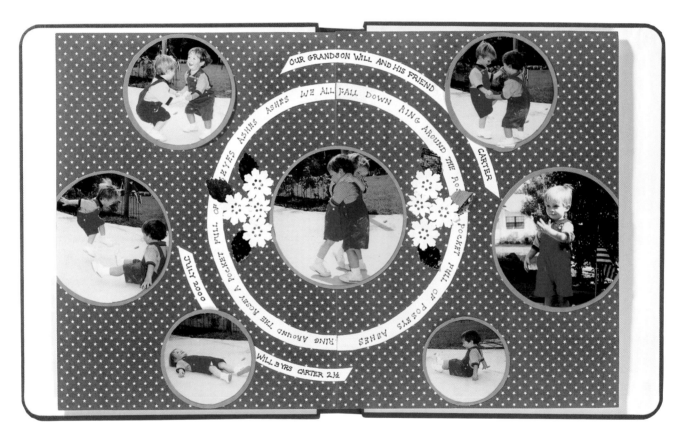

Ring Around the Rosey
ENCIRCLE PHOTOS WITH A SONG

JoAnn expanded on the idea of rings and circles when she photographed her grandson and his best friend playing "Ring Around the Rosey." First crop photos into circles; mat on solid paper. Create "rings" for title and journaling, either with a circle cutter or by tracing around a small plate. Cut one ring apart for outer ring. Layer photos and rings on patterned paper (The Paper Patch). Punch flowers (Family Treasures) from solid paper and leaves from photo scraps. Mount on page and complete with journaling.

JoAnn Petersen, Mukwonago, Wisconsin

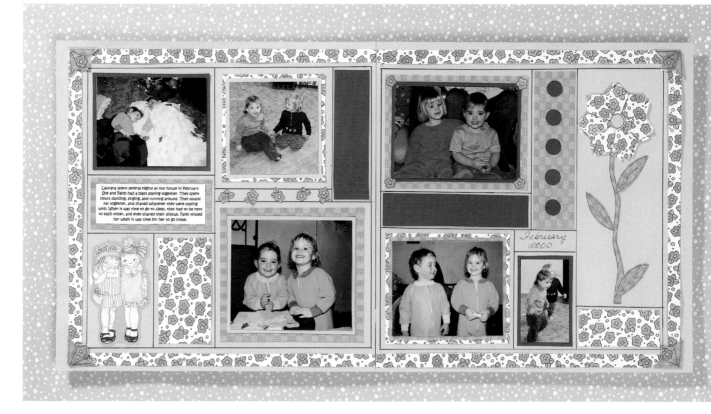

Best Friends

PAPER FOLD A FRIENDSHIP QUILT

Jennifer's daughter and best friend are just inseparable! Cut strips of patterned paper (Provo Craft); mount on cardstock border. Paper fold large flower and corner details (see page 126). Mat photos on solid, floral, and patterned (Keeping Memories Alive) papers. Mount photos, filling spaces with papers, journaling, girl die cuts (Hot Off The Press), and paper folded flower. Draw lines. Punch large circles and cut purple flowers from patterned paper; mount as shown.

Jennifer Wellborn, The Memory Tree, Las Vegas, Nevada

Forever Friends

CHALK UP A SPECIAL FRIENDSHIP

A sweet hug between friends is captured by Nicola's freshly chalked layout. Layer patterned paper (Provo Craft) over chambray cardstock (Pebbles in My Pocket) leaving a ¼" border. Double mat photo on solid and patterned (Provo Craft) paper. Freehand cut layered flowers from patterned (Provo Craft), solid, and vellum papers. Add sticker title and bees (Karen Foster). Dust blue chalk around title, photo, and flowers. Finish with pen work and journaling.

Nicola Howard, Pukekohe, New Zealand

"All About Me" Album

Another toddler favorite is an album devoted strictly to him or her, such as Anne's clever "see-through" gift album depicting qualities she loves about her son.

"It made him feel so special after a year of having a new baby brother in the spotlight," says Anne. "It reminds him that he is special and unique."

Anne simply mounted two photos on the inside front and back covers and cropped circles at the same place on each page to create the windows for her son's face to show through. Stephen's outfits (My Mind's Eye), setting, and character traits change with every turn of a page.

Anne Heyen, Glendale, New York

MORE VARIATIONS

Use photos that capture a daily routine (see pages 14-64 for ideas), character and personality traits (see page 34), social activities (see page 93 for ideas), important milestones (see page 102), favorite things (see page 123 for ideas), or a month-by-month, calendarlike growth album. Add journaling to tell the story of each photo.

You love to go to the beach. You jump the waves in the ocean and you love to DIG!

You LOVE eating watermelon. You and Daddy always share a bowl full and he takes the pits out for you.

You like the rain because you get to use your umbrella and you LOVE to jump in puddles.

You are very creative! You love to do all crafts – especially with Mommy.

You are Daddy's helper in the Kitchen. You call yourself the Little Chef.

You are our SUNSHINE!

HAPPY BIRTHDAY

Kevin and Marissa fell on the Merry-Go-Round.

Kevin's a swinging guy!

Cris's favorite was the slide.

Kevin and Marissa ready to race.

Kevin and Marissa in the bike trailer.

Taking a break from Hide-n-Seek.

Eric loved hiding in the rock.

The Park

Kevin at 2 and 3/4.

Marissa is just a month older.

Marissa would be just it wasn't for the diaper hanging on.

KEVIN, 20 MOS.

Going Places

THE REAL VOYAGE OF

DISCOVERY CONSISTS NOT

IN SEEING NEW LAND-

SCAPES, BUT IN

HAVING NEW EYES.

—MARCEL PROUST

Whether it's by plane, train, or automobile, your toddler has places to go and things to do. It might be just an impromptu Saturday jaunt to the neighborhood playground or a once-in-a-lifetime family odyssey to Disneyland. Getting there is part of the story, so look for opportunities to hike or bike or ride horses, too. Memories of travel will whet your little one's appetite for seeing the world and remind him that there is no place like home. When photographing your adventures, be sure to capture your toddler in the frame and remember it's not just the zoo elephant that's important—it's your little one marveling at the elephant.

BRANDON, 18 MOS.

THE PARK
KELLI NOTO, AURORA, COLORADO
(SEE PAGE 126)

Round 'n Round We Go!

LIGHT A FERRIS WHEEL

Create a carnival atmosphere with an "illuminated" Ferris wheel. Start with yellow patterned paper (The Crafter's Workshop). Punch jumbo blue circle and freehand cut paper strip for wheel base. Crop photos into ovals; layer to form a circle. Hole punch about 275 colored circles for "lights" after running paper through Xyron™ adhesive machine for easy mounting; adhere from center circle out toward photos for wheel arms. Adhere remaining "lights" around photos. Freehand draw and cut title letters; mount.

Idea Caroline Van Dorp,
Edmonton, Alberta, Canada

Photos Pam Klassen, Westminster, Colorado

Brookfield Zoo

FEATURE ANIMAL PAPER ART

Darla's daughter will remember her first trip to the zoo with a creative multipage layout featuring punched and paper-pieced animals. Begin with freehand cut and colored rock and water formations on backgrounds. Mat and adhere photos. GIRAFFE Freehand cut, piece, and layer with trimmed medium white heart for snout. PALM TREES Freehand cut leaves; layer over trunk trimmed with scissors. TIGER Freehand cut, piece, and layer with hand-drawn facial features. PARROTS Freehand cut, piece, and layer from colored paper. PENGUINS Punch medium heart for body, small heart for head, mini hearts for feet and nose; trim white medium heart for belly; freehand cut arms; hand-draw eyes. BEARS Punch and trim jumbo, large, and medium circles; small hearts for paws; freehand cut ears; draw eyes and noses.

Darla Stavros, Wheeling, Illinois

SHERRY'S STORY

Almost nothing in the life of a scrapbooker is more disappointing than picking up your photos from the photo lab only to discover a major disaster such as double-exposed shots. Sherry turned the tragedy of her Christmas pictures overlaying her July vacation photos into a unique page idea.

"I didn't want to discard the pictures," remembers Sherry. While flipping through the photos, her daughter Lindsay noticed a river shot with the superimposed mascot of their elementary school, a cougar. Since Sherry's son Ryan's favorite books at the time were the *I-Spy* and *Where's Waldo* series, her solution was to create a page featuring the same hide-and-seek concept.

Sherry thinks some of the pictures actually provided a hidden commentary on their life, such as a summer picture of her kids at the Royal Gorge overlapping a holiday picture of their great-grandma.

"Grandma will go sit by herself and finish her meal while we clean up because she's a little slow," says Sherry. "It's funny because I wouldn't be surprised if she was still eating when we were in Colorado!"

Sherry Baker, Florissant, Missouri

Photo Mosaics

Pieced photo mosaics are a captivating way to display just one or many related photos together on one page. The concept of photo mosaics is simple—cut your pictures into square "tiles" and arrange them as desired. The outer edges of your finished mosaic can be left intact or trimmed into a shape, such as the hamburger at left.

Playland Mosaic

Marsha's handmade hamburger fixings are the perfect showcase for a mosaic that features photos of her grandson playing at a McDonald's® Playland. To make your own mosaic hamburger to fit a 12 x 12" scrapbook page, begin by freehand cutting "veggies" and "cheese" from colored papers; trim with decorative scissors and layer onto background. Cut a 10¼" brown paper "bun" to serve as background for actual mosaic. For larger or smaller scrapbook page sizes, simply cut hamburger "fixings" larger or smaller. Then follow the steps below to create the mosaic.

Marsha Davis, Peetz, Colorado

CREATING A PHOTO MOSAIC

1 *Select photos and lay them out on paper "bun" circle, in a general format. Use a photo-safe wax pencil and a ruler to create a grid of 1" squares on the back of each photo (Figure 1), holding photo against a light source to ensure that your lines will not cut through facial features. Adjust where you draw the grid lines as necessary.*

2 *Number each square on the back of photos by row (Figure 2), numbering backward to maintain proper order when photos are flipped over.*

3 *Cut photos into 1" squares (Figure 3) and put individual photos in sandwich bags or envelopes to keep them separate.*

4 *Begin with the photo squares that feature faces, placing them in the center and working outward as desired (Figure 4), using the most interesting pieces of each photo. Do not adhere tiles yet.*

5 *Fill in the rest of the "bun" with remaining squares until the desired layout is achieved (Figure 5). Straighten squares neatly into mosaic pattern; adhere squares one at a time.*

6 *Flip "bun" over; trim away overlapping photo squares (Figure 6). Mount mosaic atop hamburger "fixings" on scrapbook page.*

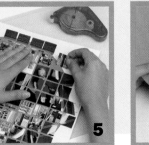

Having a Ball at Playland

CROP CIRCLES TO MIMIC A THEME

Sharon cropped playtime photos into circles to replicate the fun her grandkids had playing in a bounty of balls. Begin with red and green background. Crop photos into circles; mat some on colored paper trimmed with decorative scissors (Fiskars). Cut title banner and caption circles from yellow paper. Mat captions on layers of colored paper; trim all with decorative scissors. Draw title and lettering. Add decorative dots and dashes in black ink.

Sharon LaCroix, Orem, Utah

Rest Area

EXPAND ON ELEMENT FROM PAPER

Shauna chose an ideal sign to mat a photo of her son snoozing in the car. First, mat and trim patterned paper (Hot Off The Press) with decorative scissors (Family Treasures); layer on yellow background. Triple mat photo, leaving wide border for lettering. Freehand draw sign letters and arrow in white. Cut letters from template (Provo Craft) from patterned paper; outline in black ink. Silhouette crop road signs from paper; mount on page.

Shauna Immel, Beaverton, Oregon

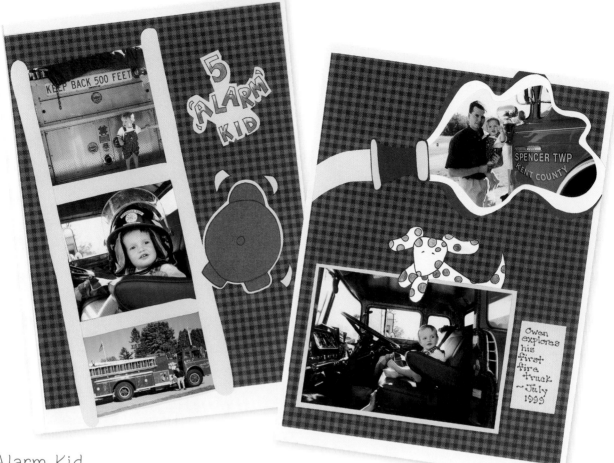

5 Alarm Kid

SHOWCASE A SPECIAL VISIT

Jennifer's son's fascination with firetrucks lands him in the driver's seat at a local fire station. Begin with plaid paper (Creative Memories) background. Cut two 11" and two 4" yellow paper strips for ladder; crop photos to fit and assemble. Freehand draw alarm; mat alarm and large photo on yellow paper. Jennifer enlarged dog sticker (Creative Imaginations) to layer behind photo. Freehand draw, cut, and assemble hose and spray; crop photo to fit. Freehand draw title letters; add flame detail. Journal on yellow paper.

Jennifer Guyor-Jowett, Saranac, Michigan

Preschool Circus

SPOTLIGHT A GREAT PERFORMANCE

Liza's choice of bright colors and friendly circus animals reflects the festive atmosphere of her son's preschool circus. Begin by layering yellow and red patterned papers (Close To My Heart) for background. Freehand draw a semicircle at page top, layer freehand cut triangles for flag banner. Silhouette crop animals from stationery (Amscan); layer with photos trimmed with corner rounder. Use performance program for title. Add silhouette-cropped photo at top and finish with journaling.

Liza Wasinger, Fairfax, Virginia

Dear Noah,

We have always enjoyed traveling to see our family, friends, and to visit new places. Mommy and Daddy went to England for our honeymoon. One day, we hope to take you there. When you were born, we decided to make you a traveler from the beginning. Your first road trip was when you where just a two months old. We went to Tennessee to visit Grandma & Grandpa Myer. A few weeks later, you had your first stay in a hotel when we went to Charleston, South Carolina for the weekend. One day, we were curious about how many miles you had traveled. We were so surprised when we discovered that you had ridden over 20,000 miles in your car seat. Some years we've gone more places than others. We thought it would be great fun to start documenting the states that you had traveled to or through. Our hope is that this travel journal will remind you of all the places you have been and the memories of getting there. One day, it will be up to you to complete the journey. We hope you that your enjoy the trip!!

Happy Trails!

Love,
Mommy
10/00

TRAVEL VARIATION

Travel can be as simple as a walk around the neighborhood or a day of running errands with Mom, with photos and journaling of what your child does, says, and sees. Or put a reverse spin on travel, by photographing and journaling about the visitors who come to see your child at home.

Travel Album

Toddlers live to go "bye-bye," whether it's across the city or across the country. Their memories of travel are often shorter than the trips themselves, which is why Monica made an album with each page representing a different state. As her family visits each state, she adds to the page. The album also incorporates postcards, memorabilia, hand-journaled state trivia, and travel photos.

"We were so surprised to discover that Noah had ridden over 20,000 miles in his car seat," writes Monica. "One day, it will be up to Noah to complete the journey. Happy trails!"

Monica Sautter, Greenwood, South Carolina

My Trip

DOCUMENT A COCKPIT TOUR

Kelly and her daughter get a close look at how to fly the friendly skies. Background cloud paper (me & my BIG ideas) provides the border. Cut decorative photo frames from patterned paper (me & my BIG ideas); crop photos to fit. Double mat remaining photos; layer on page. Double mat printed journaling. Mount airplane die cut (Ellison) and small, freehand-cut airplanes. Add title sticker letters (Provo Craft) and journal with black pen.

Kelly Angard, Highlands Ranch, Colorado

What a Character!

ADD CHARM TO THEME PHOTOS

A picture-perfect day at Disneyland resulted in magical photos of Kelly's family with colorful characters. Vibrant colors jump off of a black background bordered with cropped, colored rectangles. Crop photos into shapes and mat on solid colored paper. Feature a favorite photo over freehand cut mouse ears; mat on white paper. Silhouette crop Disney character from patterned paper (Hot Off The Press). Adhere sticker letters (Provo Craft) on title block and paper squares; detail with black pen. Mat title block on patterned paper (Hot Off The Press).

Kelly Angard, Highlands Ranch, Colorado

At the Beach

CAPTURE SANDY TEXTURE

Heather adds simple style with texture on a layout of her daughter enjoying a quiet day on a shell-filled beach. Photos are matted on complementary colors, keeping the focus on the beauty of the landscape. The star, cut from sandpaper using a template (Frances Meyer), adds a textural element. Cut title from beach photos using a template (Provo Craft); adhere onto matted paper squares. Complete page with journaling and gold ink details.

Heather Ho, Milwaukee, Wisconsin

Magical Moments

RECAPTURE SIMPLE PLEASURES

With so much going on at the Magic Kingdom®, Tina found it hard to remember every moment; so she recorded a few of her favorites on a clean, two-page spread. Begin with patterned paper backgrounds with a yellow patterned side border matted with purple patterned paper (Everafter). Freehand cut mouse ears and Mickey; mount on side border. Crop photos; mat on patterned papers. Cut title letters from patterned paper using template (Pebbles In My Pocket); mount on matted paper squares; adhere. Punch small stars and small Mickey® (All Night Media); mount at bottom of printed journaling and dot "I" in the title.

Tina Burton, Mounds, Oklahoma

Preschool & Social Activities

Everything we need to know in life, we begin to learn in preschool and other social settings. How to wait our turn. How to play well with others. When to stand up for ourselves. With the lessons come a wealth of mementos for scrapbooking: nametags, early drawings, experimental writing, and photos—lots of photos.

At Lamb's Gate Preschool
PRESERVE MEMORIES AND HANDWRITING

Memorabilia and creative journaling help Laurie capture the essence of her son's preschool days and his first attempts at writing his own name. Cut 1½" wide strips of different colored papers to fit page; adhere to top, bottom and sides of pages. Crop photos; mount. Add journaling, leaving room for memorabilia and stickers (Mrs. Grossman's).

Laurie Connolly, Mukilteo, Washington

The First Day of School
CREATE A PORTRAIT BLACKBOARD

A blackboard kit (source unknown) sets the perfect stage for Janie's son's preschool photos. Silhouette-crop child and teacher; mount at bottom corner. Mat portrait on yellow paper; attach photo corners. Add pencil (Carson-Dellosa Publishing), apple (Ellison) and title die cuts and journaling.

Janie Thomas, Blakely, Georgia

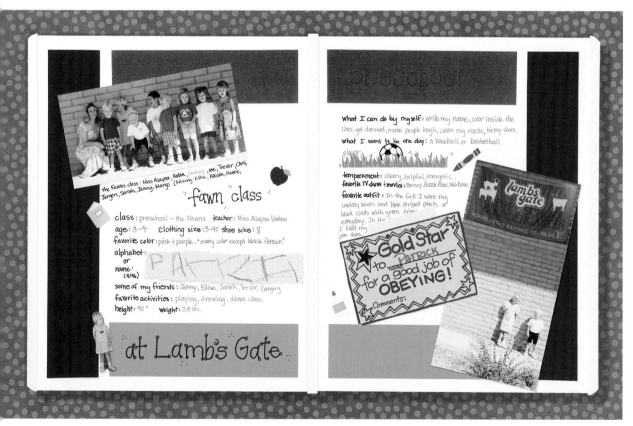

1st Trip to the Dentist

DOCUMENT DENTAL CHECK-UP

Melissa's son was a perfect patient at his first visit to the dentist, and became quite an avid brusher! Crop photos, double mat on solid paper. Print title, journaling, and date; mat on paper. Adhere dental-related stickers (Mrs. Grossman's). Layer photos and title over patterned paper (PrintWorks).

Melissa Caligiuri, Winter Park, Florida

Me, My Brush, and I

ACCENT NEW SKILL

Cindy's photos of her son brushing his teeth for the first time are surrounded by clever, hand-made die cuts, crafted to look like the real thing. Double and triple mat circle-cut photos on solid paper; mount on patterned paper (Provo Craft) background. Freehand draw title, silhouette crop words and mat. Assemble on black paper, trim to shape. Print journaling; crop with decorative scissors and mat.

Cindy Mendiola, Norwalk, California

My First Haircut

FEATURE A TINY TRIM

Nicole's daughter needed just a tiny trim for her first haircut, so Nicole did it herself and documented the process. Start by cropping and circle cutting photos. Mat on solid paper. Craft paper doll heads (Stamping Station); add detail with pens and chalk. Layer freehand-cut bow and thinly sliced paper curled into hair wisps. Print title and journaling, crop and mount. Color copy scissors; silhouette crop and mount. Save small lock of hair tied with ribbon in memorabilia pocket (3L Corp.); mount on page.

Nicole Ramsaroop, Horst, Netherlands

Beauty School Drop-Out

RECORD A SPONTANEOUS SNIP

Nicole's daughter got fed up with her hair falling over her eyes, so she took matters into her own hands and cut it off! Document a self-styled mishap by matting photos with paper and trimming with decorative scissors. Layer scissors die cut (Ellison) on photo. Adhere sticker letters (Creative Memories) for title and decorative stickers (Mrs. Grossman's) around page. Complete with journaling.

Nicole Slager, Frankfort, Illinois

Travis' First Nightmare

JOURNAL ABOUT TODDLER FEARS

Damaged film couldn't erase the memories of Jami's son's first visit to the museum, so she used
brochure clippings and lots of journaling to tell the story of why Travis had his first nightmare.
To begin, layer patterned paper (Masterpiece Studios) over yellow background.
Journal title and story with computer font (*Chiller* by Microsoft Word); crop to fit in clouds.
Crop dinosaurs from brochures; mount. Add captions in brown ink
and die cut stars (Katee's Kut-Ups) to finish.

Jami McCormick, Louisville, Colorado

Josh's Buzz

MAKE PAGE THEME A PLAY ON WORDS

Alison chronicles the story of a haircut
gone wrong when Dad tried his hand
at being a barber. The page humorously
plays on the word "buzz" with bee
stickers (Mrs. Grossman's) scattered
on the page. A freehand-cut beehive,
crafted from tan paper and detailed
with brown pen, title stickers
(Creative Memories), and journaling
complete the page.

Alison List, Jacksonville, North Carolina

First Movie

PAPER PIECE FAVORITE CHARACTERS

Chris spent many hours re-creating
characters that stand tall in her son's eyes.
Though paper piecing can take time, the
spectacular outcome is worth the effort.
To create your own paper-pieced movie
character, enlarge a coloring book page
and cut apart into pattern pieces, or trace
over lines with carbon paper onto desired
papers, cut apart, and assemble. Top the
page with a title banner that combines
movie-theme stickers (Frances Meyer)
with sticker letters (Provo Craft).

Chris Peters, Hasbrouck Heights, New Jersey

Once upon a time, not so very long ago, my dear, there was a little boy and his name was James Colin Siler.

James was ever such a good little boy and always did what his Mama told him to.... (well almost always)

One night, James's Mama told him his story, listened to his prayers and tucked him up in his ever-so-warm bed. Then she turned out the light and closed the door and James fell fast, fast asleep.

STORYBOOK VARIATIONS

Center a favorite childhood story on your child; perhaps one of the toddler favorites listed on page 23. Simply use the book's illustrations for your own illustrating inspiration and alter the text to fit your child's personality. Or, feature songs—from nursery rhymes to show tune favorites to Sunday school hymns—illustrating each with family photos that match the theme or the mood of the songs. Perhaps let your child make up his own story and help you illustrate it. It'll be the silliest story you've ever heard, and will provide great insight into your child's preschool character years from now!

James and the Moonbeam Bear

by Mommy

1986

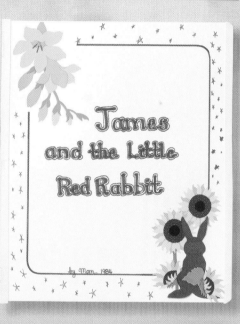

James and the Little Red Rabbit

by Mom, 1984

Storybook Album

Toddlers love to hear stories when they are featured as the main character. In fairy tale fashion, Lynnette spins many stories—each with its own title page— with her son James as the main character.

"I've always enjoyed making up children's stories and James had special ones he wanted to hear over and over again," says Lynnette. "We even act out the stories and take photos to help illustrate them. It's a fun family activity!"

Lined album pages, cropped photos, stickers, and die cuts help Lynette spin her tales with ease.

Lynnette Siler, Corona, California

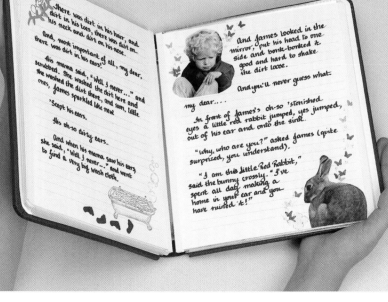

Poems & Sayings

You'll have no trouble finding photos to go with these great little sentiments for your child's scrapbook.

Every child is a different kind of little flower, and all together, they make this world a garden. —Author unknown

Children pull on our apron strings for a while, but on our heart strings forever. —Author unknown

Today I am a child.
My work is play!
—Author unknown

A mother's children are portraits of herself. —Author unknown

HOP POP. We like to hop.
We like to hop on top of pop. —Dr. Seuss, *Hop on Pop*, 1963

The Toddler Creed
If I want it, it's mine.
If I give it to you and change my mind later, it's mine.
If I can take it away from you, it's mine.
If I had it a little while ago, it's mine.
If it's mine, it will never belong to anybody else, no matter what.
If we are building something together, all the pieces are mine.
If it looks just like mine, it is mine. —Author unknown

How will our children know who they are if they don't know where they came from? —Ma in *Grapes of Wrath*

Our children are the only possessions we can take to heaven.
—Author unknown

There are no seven wonders of the world in the eyes of a child. There are seven million. —Walt Streightift

A truly rich man is one whose children run into his arms when his hands are empty. —Pilar Coolinta

All kids are gifted; some just open their packages earlier than others. —Michael Carr

Children are to be treated gently. They are like snowflakes—unique, but only here for a while. —Don Ward

The only thing worth stealing is a kiss from a sleeping child.
—Joe Hollsworth

Cleaning your house while your kids are still growing is like shoveling the walk before it stops snowing. —Phyllis Diller

My best creation is my children. —Diane von Furstenberg

You can learn many things from your children. How much patience you have, for instance. —Franklin Jones

Turn around and you're two, turn around and you're four, turn around and you're a young girl going out of my door.
—Malvina Collins, *Turn Around*, 1958

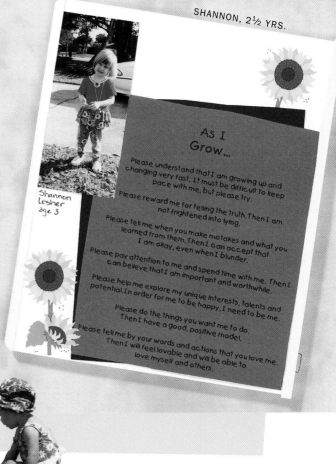

SHANNON, 2½ YRS.

Shannon
lesher
age 3

As I Grow...

Please understand that I am growing up and changing very fast. It must be difficult to keep pace with me, but please try.

Please reward me for telling the truth. Then I am not frightened into lying.

Please tell me when you make mistakes and what you learned from them. Then I can accept that I am okay, even when I blunder.

Please pay attention to me and spend time with me. Then I can believe that I am important and worthwhile.

Please help me explore my unique interests, talents and potential. In order for me to be happy, I need to be me.

Please do the things you want me to do. Then I have a good, positive model.

Please tell me by your words and actions that you love me. Then I will feel lovable and will be able to love myself and others.

EMILY, 2½ YRS.

CLAIRE, 11 MOS.

Lettering Patterns & Page Title Ideas

Use these convenient lettering patterns to add a fun finishing touch to your toddler and preschool pages. Simply photocopy the lettering pattern, scaled to the size you need, and trace onto your page in pencil using a light table or window. Retrace and color in pen color of your choice. Or make your own patterns from the page title ideas listed by theme.

A DAY IN THE LIFE
A day in our life
It's toddler time!
Just hangin' out...
Our day in review
Simple pleasures
Welcome to our zoo

MEALTIME
Finger lickin' good!
Floor food's the best
My favorite foods...

BATH
Bathing beauty
Bubble, bubble, toil and trouble...
You clean up well!

SLEEPING
Going, going, gone....
I'll sleep anywhere, any time
Rise & shine!
Sweet dreams

MINIATURE MAYHEM
Caught in the act
It's the smile that keeps me out of trouble
My name's "No No," what's yours?
Pantry raid
Spoiled rotten
The original rugrat

JUST FOR FUN
Born to be wild
Clownin' around
Drama king or queen
Kids do the darndest things
Laughter is the best medicine
Monkeyin' around
The fun starts here
The streak
You're unbelievable!

CHILD'S PLAY
Backyard fun
Beep, beep, coming through
Boy toys
Boys will be boys
Everything a girl needs
Hide-n-seek
I love my blankie...
Just a swingin'
My dollhouse
My lil' Picasso
Painting is fun
Peek-a-boo!
Slip, sliding away
Toys R Me
Vrooom...

ALL IN A DAY'S WORK
Future careers
Hard at work
It's a guy thing
Just my size
Mommy's or Daddy's little helper
Monkey see, monkey do

FAMILY
A hug to remember
Brotherly love
Count your blessings
Family reunion
Family ties
Grandma's garden
Home, sweet home
It takes somebody special to be a daddy
It's all relative
Kissing cousins
Love lives here
Mommy's angel
My Grandpa & me
Sibling rivalry at its best
Sisters are forever
We are family!

FRIENDS
Best buddies
Best of times
Forever friends
Friendship blooms
Girlfriends forever
My new friends
Two peas in a pod

GOING PLACES
A day at the zoo
Do you see what I see?
Farm fun
Gone fishing
Mall adventure
On the go
Picnic at the park
Planes, trains, and automobiles
Pumpkin patch
State fair

TRIPS & VACATIONS
Away we go
Beach boys
Life's a beach
Road rules
Sea princess
Wish you were here

nothing a little
SOAP AND WATER

won't cure

I spy...

UH-OH!

100% GIRL

Artist
AT WORK

ROLLING ROLLING ROLLING ROLLING

NO! NO! NO!

Here Comes
TROUBLE

BOYS AT WORK   ALL BOY

Project Patterns

Use these helpful patterns to complete specific scrapbook pages featured in this book. Photocopy and enlarge the patterns as needed to fit your photos and/or page size.

AUSTYN POTTY TRAINING, PAGE 108

PLAYTIME, PAGE 42

NIGHT NIGHT ZORYANA, PAGE 21

ENLARGE AND REDUCE AS NEEDED TO CREATE DIFFERENT-SIZED RINGS.

PLAYTIME, PAGE 42

PLAYTIME, PAGE 42

I LOVE TO EAT, PAGE 25

WHEN THE MOMMY CAT'S AWAY, PAGE 36

Interactive Photo Paper Piecing Patterns

To make your own interactive photo paper-pieced designs, photocopy and enlarge or reduce the patterns below to fit your selected photo. Cut the pattern pieces apart, transfer pieces to colored papers, and cut out. Reassemble all elements, adding a silhouette-cropped photo to complete the design.

PAGE 43

PAGE 48

PAGE 95

PAGE 32

PAGE 51

PAGE 15

PAGE 58

PAGE 52

PAGE 69

PAGE 128

PAGE 81

PAGE 67

Charts

Our ready-made charts make it easy to begin a family tree, favorite things, or growth scrapbook page. Simply photocopy and enlarge to 115% (for an 8½ x 11" page) or 130% (for a 12 x 12" page), color as desired, and add cropped photos and journaling.

My Family Tree